ECONOMICS FACT AND FICTION

Introduction:

This book is written as food for thought by those who can think above and beyond sophomoric logic, reasoning, and conclusion; and those who can determine the difference between economic and political facts as opposed to economic and political fiction.

The numerical and statistical data may not be completely accurate, but the economic and political points that the data support are valid.

Author: Charles H. Meter
Copyright © by Charles H. Meter 2013
All Rights Reserved

CHAPTER I: A Bit of History…….…..…..4

CHAPTER II: Economic Facts……………...5

Chapter III: Production and Consumption of Wealth……………………………..……8

CHAPTER IV: Production and Consumption……………………………..…18

CHAPTER V: Creditor Nations vs. Debtor Nations………….…..…………………….....21

CHAPTER VI: The Economic Condition of the United States…………..……………….…..24

CHAPTER VII: Money and Its Relation to the Economy (Coin and currency vs. checkbook money)……………………..…….……………29

CHAPTER VIII: Corporations and Their Effect on the Economy……………………..………...…….33

CHAPTER IX: Non-Profit Corporations………..37

CHAPTER X: Creditor Nations versus Debtor Nations……………………………………..40

CHAPTER I: A Bit of History

Economics has been called the dismal science. However, economics is neither dismal nor a science, but it is the basic life support system for all living things on the Planet Earth.

First, there are only two real economic activities: production and consumption. Other economic activities are for the most part activities schemed up by men in order for them to obtain their livelihood from the production of others. For example, insurance activities do not produce any wealth but consume a lot of other people's resources/wealth. Banks and banking activities do not produce any wealth, but consume a lot of other people's resources/wealth. There is a multitude of other activities that consume wealth but do not produce an equitable amount of wealth in return.

When man first evolved or was created, he had to have food, water, shelter and perhaps some clothing. All of these were produced by nature, and man lived on what nature provided, much the same way that other animals lived. In the very beginning, economics was a system of production and consumption. Nature produced and man consumed.

The same is true today--nature produces, people produce, and people consume.

CHAPTER II: Economic Facts

Directly or collectively:

1) All wealth in the world is owned by people.

2) Nothing can be consumed until it has been produced.

3) Nothing can be produced until it has been paid for by someone.

4) Economic entities:
   a. A person
   b. A family
   c. A village
   d. A town
   e. A city
   f. A county
   g. A state
   h. A nation
   i. The world
   j. A corporation
   k. Minor entities such as clubs, schools, churches, charities, foundations, etc.

5) You or anyone can only borrow wealth from an economic entity that has a surplus of wealth.

A surplus of wealth is defined as wealth that the owner does not need for his current use.

6) If any economic entity produces or otherwise obtains more wealth than he consumes, he will have a surplus. If he consumes more wealth than he produces or otherwise obtains, he will have a deficit. If he consumes the same amount of wealth that he produces, he will have neither a surplus nor a deficit. If any entity consumes more than it produces, it must borrow the difference from an entity that has a surplus.

7) The economic system is always in balance. That is, that debt is always equal to credit and vice versa. However, I must add here that manmade gimmicks and schemes try to upset this balance by taking credits (i.e., worthy assets) from the system and replacing them with worthless or partially worthless assets. This keeps the books in balance, but the worthy assets have been stolen by someone, usually management, and placed in their accounts,

leaving someone with the loss/debt. That is exactly what caused the financial meltdown of 2008/2009. Banks and financial institutions had their books in balance, but their worthy assets (i.e., cash and other liquid assets) had been siphoned off (stolen) and replaced by so-called toxic assets in the form of worthless or partially worthless mortgages and other worthless loans.

CHAPTER III: Production and Consumption of Wealth

All economic entities consume wealth, but many economic entities or activities do not produce any wealth or they produce less than they consume. Some examples of activities that consume much more wealth than they produce are the following: wars and the preparation for war (i.e., the production of war materials and equipment), professional sports such as golf, baseball, hockey, auto racing, basketball, football, soccer, tennis, etc.), the entire entertainment and advertisement activities such as talk radio. You might say that these activities provide information and entertainment. Yes, I agree, but nevertheless these activities do not produce any wealth and we here in the United States are being entertained right into the poorhouse. If, and that is a big IF, the United States could reduce or halt these activities, the national debt would be paid off within a very short time. Why? Because the people, and that includes all United States citizens, would not be spending their wealth on non-productive activities and would amass a surplus.

It is the people who are the government of these United States of America. Remember from the Constitution, "do ordain and establish this Government of the people, by the people, and for the people." It is the people, citizens of these United States, who owe the national debt and who eventually must repay the debt. Also, for the most part, it is the people of the country who own the national debt in the form of treasury bonds, notes and bills. These debt certificates are all the same except for their length of time to maturity. Other countries/nations or foreign entities own some of the debt. China is the current largest owner of about $1.4 trillion, Japan is the next largest foreign owner at about $800 billion, the UK/England is the third largest debt owner at about $350 billion (the UK includes all Caribbean banking centers and Channel Islands), Hong Kong owns about $90 billion, Taiwan owns about $80 billion, Switzerland owns about $75 billion, Brazil owns about $125 billion, Russia owns about $140 billion, Luxembourg owns about $105 billion, Egypt, Israel, Italy, Netherlands, Norway and Thailand combined own about $125 billion, Germany owns about $50 billion, France, India, Korea, Mexico, Singapore and Turkey combined own about $210 billion, Belgium, Canada, Chile, Colombia, Malaysia, the Philippines and Sweden combined own about $90 billion, the oil exporting countries of Algeria, Bahrain, Ecuador, Gabon, Indonesia, Iran, Iraq, Kuwait, Libya, Nigeria, Oman, Qatar, Saudi Arabia, United Arab Emirates and Venezuela combined own about $200 billion, all others own about $160 billion.

You may ask how the government of the United States could possibly be in debt to Israel, Iraq, Taiwan, Kuwait, the Philippines, Germany, France, Turkey, Mexico and many others when we have provided aid in billions of dollars to these countries for many years, as well as providing for their defense and freedom. The total debt held by foreign interests is currently about $4 trillion.

The answer to your question is that the debt held by these foreign interests is not entirely or even mostly owned by the governments of these nations, but is mostly owned by the banking institutions, insurance companies and other financial and corporate institutions headquartered within these countries. Also, these foreign banks, corporations and financial institutions are partly, and in some cases mostly, owned by American (U.S.) citizens and corporations. For instance, American corporations and individuals own a great amount of the wealth of China, Japan, Taiwan, Israel and most of the others. So it is difficult to say just how much of the national debt is actually owned by foreign interests. The banks, insurance companies, corporations and other financial institutions hold U.S. Treasury bonds, notes and bills issued to their accounts, but it is almost impossible to say who the individuals are who actually own these entities. Remember that all wealth in the world is owned by people.

The total national debt is about $15 trillion. Of this amount, foreign entities own about $4 trillion worth, which leaves $11 trillion worth that is directly owned by U.S. entities. Of the $11 trillion owned by U.S. entities, the Social Security Trust Fund owns about $3 trillion. The remaining $8 trillion of debt is owned by various American banks, insurance companies, corporations and foundations, charities, churches, towns, villages, cities, counties, states, clubs and individuals.

You have heard many times that we, the government of the United States, are creating a debt for our children and grandchildren to pay back. On the surface this statement seems to be logical and truthful, but it is one of the biggest lies that has ever been concocted by politicians and others such as radio talk show hosts. The truth of the matter is that as a society of we the people in the here and now, it is impossible for us to create a debt for some future entity to pay. Remember, for every debit there is an equal credit. Now, who owes the debt? It is we the people, and who owns the debt? It is we the people. You might ask what about the debt that is owned by foreign entities, and I submit to you that American/U.S. entities own more foreign wealth than U.S. wealth owned by foreign entities. If not, it is close to a wash.

Now comes the clincher, as to our children and grandchildren. It depends on whose children and grandchildren they happen to be. If they are the children or grandchildren of those who own the debt, then they will not only receive repayment and interest, but they will also owe their share of the debt. If they are the children and grandchildren who do not own a part of the debt, then they will owe their part of the debt to the children and grandchildren of the owners of the debt. The wealthy U.S. people for the most part own the debt, but every U.S. citizen owes the debt. As a society of we the people as a whole, not only owe the debt, but we also own the debt in the form of Treasury bonds, notes and bills. Until we as a society of we the people can borrow wealth from Mars or Jupiter, it is impossible for us in the here and now to create a debt for our children and grandchildren to pay. As a society, we owe the debt to ourselves.

You also often hear statements from politicians and others that there is no money in the Social Security Trust Fund and that the Trust Fund money has been spent on other government activities. This is another big lie. Yes, the government/Treasury has borrowed the Trust Fund assets and replaced these assets with Treasury bonds. In other words, the Social Security Trust Fund has bought about $3 trillion worth of U.S. Treasury bonds that are backed by the full faith and credit of the United States of America, the same as all other

Treasury bonds, notes and bills, regardless of who owns them. All of these Treasury debt instruments pay interest to the owners regardless of who owns them. Not one penny of Social Security Trust Fund money has been spent on anything except Social Security.

I also submit to you that there is no money, or very little, in your bank account, your insurance account, your brokerage account or any other credit account that you may own. If you deposit ten thousand dollars in your bank account, the bank credits your account with ten thousand dollars, but almost immediately loans 86% of your deposit to others. The bank is required to keep only 14% of your deposit in reserve, which is mostly deposited in the Federal Reserve Bank on which your bank can withdraw funds or borrow funds as they need them.

Nearly all financial economic activities are executed with credit and debit instruments, and rarely does any cash ever change hands. For example, if you wanted to buy a new automobile and you went to the auto dealer and picked the auto you want, and the negotiated price was $25 thousand, and you had at least $25 thousand in credit in your bank account, you would not draw out $25 thousand in cash and take it to the auto dealer to pay for the automobile. You would write a check on your account or get a cashier's check to pay for the automobile, and no cash money would change hands. The same is true in the big business world where billions of dollars' worth of many different forms of wealth is exchanged every day, and no cash or money changes hands. For instance, the New York Stock Exchange buys and sells billions of dollars' worth of stock every work day.

At this point, I must explain some of the points that I have extolled. First, I have stated that all wealth in the world is owned by people, which is a completely true statement. However, you may ask about the wealth that is owned by governments, corporations, charities, foundations, clubs, churches and other entities. The answer is that this wealth is still owned by people or groups of people indirectly, but is not under the control of the individuals who share ownership of this wealth. In other words, we the people of the United States of America own the government of these United States and all of its assets, but no one citizen or groups of citizens can sell their share of ownership of this wealth. We do, however, have the use of a great amount of this wealth in the form of public buildings, highways, bridges, airports, waterways, airways, national parks and a host of many other benefits and services provided by our federal government.

The same principle is true of the other entities over which individuals do not have direct control of their share of assets. For instance, if you are a member of the Catholic Church, you cannot sell your share that you own in the Vatican. Likewise, as a United States citizen, you cannot sell the share that you own in the U.S. capitol building or the share that you own in Yellowstone National Park, etc.

CHAPTER IV: Production and Consumption

Facts:

1) Everything that is consumed must first be produced.

2) Everything that is produced will be consumed, except perhaps diamonds which someone said are forever.

There are two kinds of production: necessary production and unnecessary production. Necessary production is the production of food, clothing shelter, electrical energy, fuel for heating, transportation and several other things that enhance our modern day lives. Necessary production is self-explanatory and includes most of the products and things that sensible people and other economic entities use and consume in their everyday lives.

Unnecessary production is the production of those things that consume enormous amounts of wealth but do not create an equitable amount of wealth in return. Incidentally, these production activities are the root cause of inflation. Some examples of unnecessary production are the following:

1) NASCAR races.
2) Golf tournaments.
3) Horse races.
4) Professional football.
5) Professional basketball.
6) Professional hockey.
7) Professional soccer.
9) Motion pictures - movies.
10) Television programs.
11) Radio talk shows.
12) Mountain climbing.
13) Yacht races.
14) University sports
15) Concerts.
16) Tourism.
17) A plethora of other activities too numerous to mention that consume a tremendous amount of wealth but do not produce an equitable amount of wealth in return.

There are also two kinds of consumption: necessary consumption and unnecessary consumption. Necessary consumption is self-explanatory and includes the consumption of the things that are necessarily produced.

Unnecessary consumption is the big culprit in our (United States of America) economic system. We United States citizens consume enormous amounts of unnecessary things; i.e., entertainment, which in the final analysis is a waste of our national and individual wealth.

I do not mean to denigrate all sports and entertainment activities, but we Americans indulge ourselves in far too much and too many of these frivolous wealth-consuming activities. Americans seem to have an insatiable appetite for sports and all other forms of entertainment. Too many and too much of these unnecessary wealth-consuming activities are just that--too many and too much.

CHAPTER V: Creditor Nations vs. Debtor Nations

The following list of nations is for the present creditor nations, defined as nations that possess more assets/wealth than they need for their own current use.

1) Switzerland
2) Sweden
3) Finland
4) Norway
5) Denmark
6) Saudi Arabia
7) Kuwait
8) Brazil
9) Venezuela
10) Argentina
11) China
12) Japan
13) Germany
14) Russia
15) Taiwan
16) Netherlands
17) Canada
18) Belgium
19) Chile, and a few others

You should notice that most of these creditor nations support only one or two national sports activities. For most, it is what we call soccer and they call football. You should also note that they do not support a huge motion picture industry or equivalent activities such as NASCAR racing, and many other sports or entertainment activities. All of these creditor nations combined do not support nearly as many of the wealth-wasting and consuming activities as does the United States of America. They do not have an NFL, an AFL, an NBA, an NBL, an ABL, an AHL, an ABA, or many of the other wealth-consuming activities supported by we the people of the United States of America.

Debtor Nations: Defined as nations that consume more wealth than they possess or produce.

Some examples of current debtor nations are:

1) The United States of America
2) Greece
3) Spain
4) Italy
5) Haiti
6) Several of the poor African, Central American, Southern Asia and South American nations

Except for the United States and Italy, one should note that these debtor nations are not highly industrialized nations, nor do they have the capacity to produce a multitude of goods and services in excess of their needs; hence, their consumption of more wealth than they produce.

One should also note that the creditor nations do not waste their wealth on auto racing, professional sports and other unnecessary economic production and consumption activities.

CHAPTER VI: The Economic Condition of the United States

The United States (i.e., all U.S. citizens) is in its current economic limbo because U.S. citizens would rather waste their wealth on all of the unnecessary production and consumption activities that I have listed in Chapter III rather than use their wealth to pay for the services and benefits that they expect from their various levels of government. The cure for this limbo condition is for all levels of government that need more revenue to meet their expenses is to levy a relatively high tax on most of these unnecessary consumption activities.

For instance, I would suggest that the federal government levy a tax of at least 40% on all tickets for attendance at all professional sports and entertainment activities. Most of these activities are engaged in interstate commerce and should be taxed at the federal level. The states, counties and cities should also tax these unnecessary activities as needed.

Now, you point out to me that all of these unnecessary activities provide jobs and income for a host of people who pay taxes and contribute to the welfare of their country, etc. I must remind you, however, that the product they produce is fleeting and ephemeral. When you use your wealth to buy entertainment, you have bought something that you cannot eat, drink, wear, drive, ride, take to the bank or sell to someone else. In the final analysis, U.S. citizens do not want to pay for the expenses of the federal government, but are willing to waste their wealth on unnecessary activities that provide them with little or nothing in return.

Most people (U.S. citizens) believe that they are taxed too much, but in fact they are taxed too little. For instance, let us set up some hypothetical conditions regarding federal governmental services as opposed to private enterprise services. Currently, air traffic control is provided by the federal government as well as most airports and facilities.

Let us suppose that the federal government, in order to help balance the budget, decided to stop providing air traffic control and other airport facilities and told the airline companies that as of a certain date, they would have to provide their own air traffic control and other airport facilities. Now the airline companies would have to charge considerably more for their services. Consequently airline passengers would foot the bill for air traffic control as well as for airports and airport facilities that are now paid for by federal taxes. I also could say that I never use commercial airlines; therefore, why should I allow my tax money to be used to support the travel expenses of others?

There are also many individuals, companies and others who own airplanes, yachts and boats who use federal-provided facilities. If a privately owned airplane has an emergency and has to ditch the aircraft at sea, the Coast Guard (a federal agency) stands ready to dispatch a rescue Coast Guard cutter and/or rescue helicopters to the aid of the downed aircraft, its pilots and passengers mostly at taxpayer expense. The same is true for yacht and boat owners who are in danger of sinking.

Now let us suppose that the federal government, in order to help balance the budget, decided that it would stop providing air and sea search and rescue services as of a certain date and that airlines, private aircraft owners, yacht and boat owners would have to provide for their own search and rescue services and would be at their own peril if they encountered an emergency situation at sea or any other venue. I again could say, as well as many other U.S. taxpayers, that I do not own an airplane or a yacht or boat. Therefore, why should I allow my tax money to be spent on air and sea search and rescue operations?

There are a good many people who use very few federal governmental services. The most wealthy U.S. citizens use more governmental services than the less wealthy U.S. Citizens; hence, they should pay more taxes. There are some governmental services that practically all U.S. citizens use. To name a few: food safety by the Department of Agriculture, prescription drugs, and many over-the-counter drug safety services by the federal drug agency, the building and maintenance of bridges, highways, waterways and public buildings, building and maintaining flood control dams and levees, etc., plus a plethora of other services and facilities.

CHAPTER VII: Money and Its Relation to the Economy (Coin and currency vs. checkbook money)

There are two kinds of money--real money by definition is coin and currency that is the minted coins and the printed Federal Reserve notes. This money accounts for approximately only 5% of the total money in circulation at any given time, and this has been the case for the last 40 years. As an economic society, we could exist without a supply of coin and currency.

Before the year 1950, when most people went shopping, they took cash/currency with them to pay for the things they bought. Since the advent of the credit card and the debit card and the necessity for most people to maintain a checking account, very few people carry enough cash to pay for the things they buy. Hence, the need for a large supply of coin and currency is no longer necessary. Most people, however, need to maintain a bank account to cover their credit card, debit card and the personal checks they write or charge during the month or other time period.

Much of what I have explained above refers to both coin, currency and checkbook money. To explain further about checkbook money and how it is created, I will explain in the following hypothetical example:

Let us suppose that Chevron Oil Company wants to open a new oil well field and it needs ten drilling rigs and new equipment, plus personnel and all that goes with this new endeavor. Also let us suppose that Chevron needs a bank loan for 50% of the cost of developing this new oil field. The total cost is estimated at $4 billion, and they apply to their service bank for a loan of $2 billion. The bank knows that Chevron is a credit-worthy customer and has always repaid its loans on time with interest. The bank is eager to make the loan but, as with most banks, it does not have $2 billion readily available to loan. It does, however, have a way to obtain $2 billion worth of checkbook money, and this is the way that it is done.

The service bank goes to its servicing Federal Reserve Bank and presents its proposal to loan Chevron $2 billion. The Federal Reserve Bank reviews the Chevron loan request, and knowing that Chevron is a credit-worthy borrower, it approves the loan. Now Chevron's servicing bank can set up a Chevron account for the $2 billion on which Chevron can write checks or use when needed to develop its new oil wells.

Note that no cash money is used in this loan deal and it is a win, win, win, win transaction. Chevron wins because now it can expand its oil business, the Chevron service bank wins because it will collect interest on the loan, and the Federal Reserve Bank wins because it will receive its portion of the interest from the Chevron servicing bank, and the economy will win because Chevron will have created thousands of new jobs, not only in the oil field development, but also in hundreds of supply and support activities. Note that no new money is printed or put in circulation, and that $2 billion is added to the economy with only the stroke of a pen, or in this modern world, with only credit and debit entries on a computer keyboard. Once Chevron has used the $2 billion loan and eventually repaid the loan with interest, everything is cleared and we are now back at square one. Thousands of these types of financial transactions (loans) are consummated every week between the banking system and various economic entities.

CHAPTER VIII: Corporations and Their Effect on the Economy

Corporations by law can sue or be sued, and on that basis and other peripheral rights, the Supreme Court has determined that corporations are people. However, they are not people as in "We the People." Corporations are owned by people, usually the common stockholders. Now, if corporations are people and they are owned by other people (i.e., stockholders), the stockholders are guilty of breaking the anti-slavery laws which prohibit people from owning other people. I say that with tongue in cheek, but it makes as much sense as does the Supreme Court's decision that "corporations are people."

Corporations are the bane of our United Sates political and economic systems. Corporations should not be allowed to donate or otherwise give away corporate assets. Why? Because corporate assets belong to the stockholders and not to the CEOs, CFOs, COOs, nor to the Boards of Directors.

I am speaking here about publicly held corporations, not private corporations. As a common stockowner of several publicly traded corporations, I do not want my share of assets to be donated to political parties, nor to politicians nor to any other cause, including charities.

Corporate CEOs, CFOs, COOs are employees of the corporation for which they work, and as such should work for agreed-upon salaries. It should be unlawful for corporations to grant bonuses or stock options to any employee of a publicly traded corporation, and the laws of these United States should so state. Why? Because the assets of a corporation belong to the common stockholders and not to the managers or to the boards of directors. As the laws and regulations now stand, corporate managers and boards of directors have a license to steal the corporate assets belonging to the stockholders. A few changes to corporate laws and regulations could correct this obscene and unfair situation.

Corporations are guilty of the destruction of our American manufacturing base. They have exported American jobs and technology to other countries, and then to make matters worse, have imported their foreign-made products back into the United States. Our textile industry is a mere fraction of what it was at the mid twentieth century, and represents the loss of millions of manufacturing jobs. Our electronics and electrical appliance industries are practically non-existent. All one has to do is look at the label on almost any manufactured product and you will find that a large number of labels will say "made in China, made in Japan, made in Taiwan, made in Italy, made in Indonesia" or some other foreign country. The export of these manufacturing jobs is the reason why we in the United States have a high unemployment rate, and why we have had a severe recession for the last five years (2007-2012).

In the final analysis, corporations have no sense of loyalty to the United States of America, nor do they possess any degree of morality.

CHAPTER IX: Non-Profit Corporations

The name "non-profit corporations" is the most egregious misnomer that has ever been distributed for literary use. Non-profit corporations identify themselves (and I use the term "themselves" loosely) as non-profit to escape certain taxes and to avoid liability lawsuits against their employees or their members.

Non-profit corporations include charities, foundations, credit unions, various health insurance companies, clubs, activities that call themselves associations, etc. Some of these so-called non-profit activities pay their managers and directors (i.e., CEOs, CFOs, COOs) very high salaries, many in the hundreds of thousands per year and some in the millions of dollars per year. Usually the larger the organization, the higher the executive compensation.

The most egregious problem with non-profit corporations is that they are not required by law or regulation to report how much compensation their executives, managers or directors are paid. Members of credit unions, who in fact are the owners of their credit union, cannot obtain what compensation CEOs or other management personnel receive. They will be told that is proprietary information and is not available. The same is true for most other non-profit corporations or other so-called non-profit organizations.

Many of these non-profit organizations have hundreds of millions of dollars of income every year, but they spend it on expansion (i.e., more credit union branches, higher compensation to management). Most of the non-profit organizations are allowed to add wealth (money) to their reserves (i.e., non-profit insurance companies, various charities and foundations) without incurring a tax liability. Executives and managers pay taxes on their income; however, many of these management personnel receive expense accounts and other perquisites such as attendance at a weeklong seminar in Hawaii, Paris or Rome. Other perqs may include use of an automobile, corporate aircraft, apartments in the heart of New York City, use of vacation sites, etc., on the value of which they pay no tax.

The things that I have mentioned herein are the reasons that non-profits have no bottom line profit. All income is expensed to corporate operations. To be fair, I should mention that executives and management personnel may incur a tax liability on some of the perquisites they receive, but in most cases these taxes are not collected because these employees of the non-profit corporations can say that the perqs they received were required for the execution of their corporate duties.

CHAPTER X: Creditor Nations versus Debtor Nations

Why is China a creditor nation? The answer to that question is that China and its people do not waste their wealth on non-essential consumption such as NASCAR races, professional sports, concerts, golf tournaments, etc. Other creditor nations such as Japan, Brazil, Switzerland, Sweden, Germany, Finland, Norway, Russia, Denmark and others exhibit the same behavior. All creditor nations produce more wealth than they consume. All debtor nations consume more wealth than they produce. Hence, creditor nations have excess wealth to loan, and all debtor nations must borrow their shortfall between what they produce and what they consume.

The rise and fall of empires has always been due to the power of production (rise) and the ease and comfort of obscene consumption (fall). I would recommend that economists of the world focus their attention on the two true economic functions of